● Complete each sentence.
Circle the word you would use.

clock   sock   shoe

1. I can't find the other ___ .

shell   pail   ·   ship

2. What is in this ___ ?

stone   paper   rope

3. He will cut the ___ .

scarf   scout   glove

4. Alma has a red ___ .

Review: Decoding/Phonics (Using Letter Sounds and Context)   CAROUSELS
Preintroduce the following new words that appear in the directions: *complete, sentence, circle, use.*

Houghton Mifflin Reading, 1989 Edition

1

1

- ○ coat
- ○ count
- ○ cut

- ○ way
- ○ were
- ○ who

- ○ try
- ○ street
- ○ tree

- ○ does
- ○ dog
- ○ dark

2

- ○ went
- ○ wait
- ○ when

- ○ paint
- ○ plant
- ○ pound

- ○ when
- ○ who
- ○ won't

- ○ walk
- ○ while
- ○ well

3

- ○ came
- ○ call
- ○ roll

- ○ if
- ○ of
- ○ or

- ○ four
- ○ sound
- ○ found

- ○ his
- ○ him
- ○ her

4

- ○ short
- ○ store
- ○ start

- ○ every
- ○ each
- ○ eat

- ○ feel
- ○ fell
- ○ family

- ○ these
- ○ three
- ○ their

Review: Vocabulary Test
Find number 1. Look at the words in the first box. Find the word *count*. Mark the space for the word. (Continue in this manner, pronouncing the words to be tested.)

CAROUSELS

Houghton Mifflin Reading, 1989 Edition

● Read each question.
Underline the answers.

1.

What can swim?

a fish   a boy
a tree   a turtle

2.

What can you play with?

a kite   a teddy bear
a cat   a walk

3.

What can you put on?

a coat   a boat
a hat   a house

4.

What can you eat?

a biscuit   a window
a story   a sandwich

Review: Comprehension (Categorizing)   CAROUSELS
Preintroduce the following new words that appear in the directions: *question, underline, answers.*

Houghton Mifflin Reading, 1989 Edition

3

● Read the story.
Then read each summary.
Circle the better one, **a** or **b**.

Jennie went for a walk.
Her dog, Reggie, went with her.
While she walked, Jennie saw many things.
She saw four boys playing with a boat.
She saw a big cat in a window.
She saw some children flying kites.
After her walk, Jennie went home.
She painted a picture of her walk.

a. Jennie went for a walk.
Her dog, Reggie, went with her.
She saw some children flying kites.

b. Jennie went for a walk.
She saw many things.
She painted a picture of the things.

Review: Reference and Study (Summarizing)   CAROUSELS
Preintroduce the following new words that appear in the directions: *summary, better.*

4

Houghton Mifflin Reading, 1989 Edition

1.

_____

2. The juice is on the **tray**.

_____

3. He will bring the __m___l__.

4. Look at all the __h_____!

_____

● Circle the word you would use
to complete each sentence.
For the last one, mark the space
for the answer.

1. stay   state   stack

     I'll ____ here while you swim.

2. pole   pile   pail

     Let's put some more in the ____.

3. safe   sand   sail

     That boat has a red ____!

★

Do you think it will ____ now?

   ◯ rain
   ◯ rope
   ◯ rang

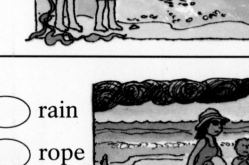

Decoding/Phonics: Sound Association for *ai, ay*
Preintroduce the following new words that appear in the directions: *last, mark, space.*

CAROUSELS

Houghton Mifflin Reading, 1989 Edition

● Read this story.

Then print the answers to the questions.

Mrs. Fox is a nice woman.

Sometimes we skate to the library
to read.

But it's raining today.

So we will look after Ben.

Ben is Mrs. Fox's cat.

She'll give Ben something to eat.

She'll give him his water, too.

Then I'll give him his play mouse!

1. Who is Mrs. Fox?

She is a

2. Why can't the boy and Mrs. Fox skate today?

It is

3. What does the boy give Ben?

He gives Ben

Vocabulary: "Beatrice"
Preintroduce the following new word that appears in the directions: *print*. Tell the children that answers have
been started to help them and that they should trace over the dotted lines.

CAROUSELS

● Think about "Beatrice."

Read each question.

Print the answer.

Use the words in the box.

Henry	Beatrice	Alfred

1. Who had work to do at the library?

_____

_____

_____

2. Who didn't want to go to the library?

_____

_____

_____

3. It was story time in the children's room.
Who was the mouse in the story?

_____

_____

_____

4. Who didn't want to go home?

_____

_____

_____

Comprehension: "Beatrice"   CAROUSELS

Houghton Mifflin Reading, 1989 Edition

● Read each sentence.
Then circle the picture that goes
with that sentence.

1. Jed got on the **scale.**

2. The soup is on the **stove.**

3. Its **stuffing** is coming out!

4. The **score** is 2 to 1.

5. Beatrice is on the **stage.**

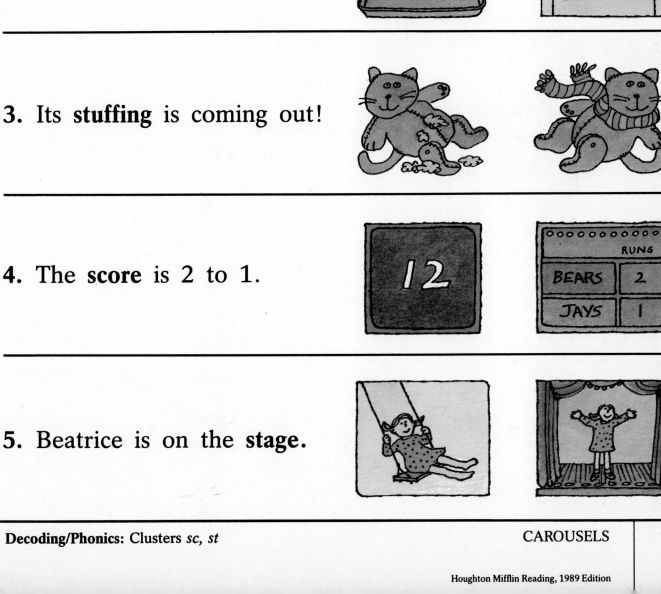

● Find the surprise.

Put your pencil on the dot by **a**.

Draw a line from **a** to **b**.

Continue all the way to **z**!

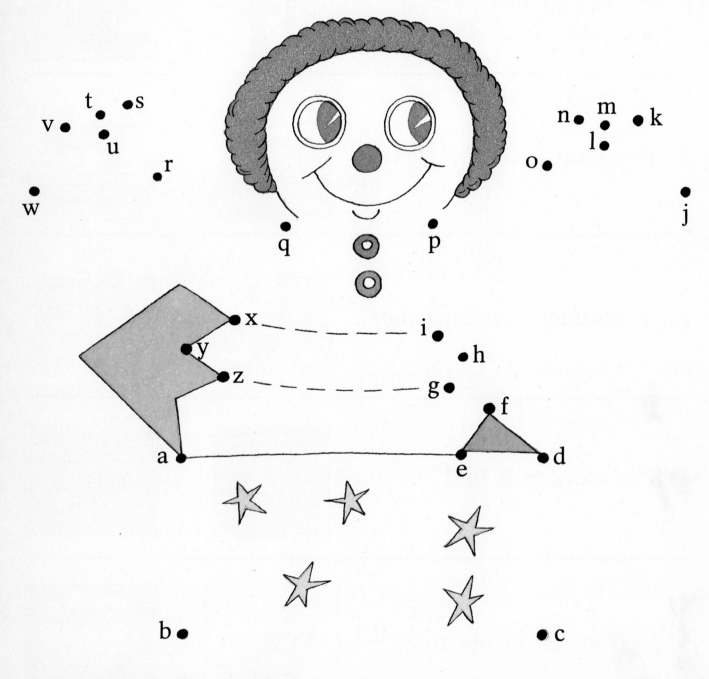

● Now color the surprise.

Decoding: Alphabetical Order   CAROUSELS
Preintroduce the following new words that appear in the directions: *dot, from, color, continue*.

order

None

letters

alphabet

● Print a word to complete each sentence.
Use the words in the box.

_____

_____

Ira will make _____ soup.

_____

_____

He has all the _____ .

Will Ira eat the letters in

_____

_____

alphabetical _____ ?

_____

_____

_____ of us would do that!

● Read the words.
Then print the words
in alphabetical order.

Reggie

Susan

Jenny

_____

1. _____

_____

2. _____

_____

3. _____

★ Read the words.
Find the word that comes
first in alphabetical order.
Mark the space for the answer.

◯ rabbit

◯ pig

◯ turtle

● Read each sentence.

Answer the question below it.

Print your answer on the line.

| **How many?** | 1 | 2 | 3 | 4 |

1. Jed has a cat, fish, dog, and turtle.

   How many pets does Jed have? ____

2. Reggie has a frog, catfish, and rabbit.

   How many pets does Reggie have? ____

3. John got fish, soup, oranges,

   and juice at the store.

   How many things did John get? ____

4. Mary got fish soup, oranges,

   and juice at the store.

   How many things did Mary get? ____

5. Mary Ana, Max, and Ben are in the play.

   How many children are in the play? ____

● Read the play.

Finish the sentences to show the order of what was said.

Print your answers in the lines.

Duck: Who's there?

Bear: Boo.

Duck: Boo who?

Bear: Don't cry, Duck!

_____

_____

_____

Duck asked, _____

_____

_____

Bear said, _____

_____

_____

_____ asked Duck.

_____

_____

_____ said Bear.

It is fun to make bread.
You mix flour, water, and
other things to make dough.
When you bake the dough,
you get bread.

The library is a nice place.
There are many books there.
Some books have stories in them.
Other books tell you about things.
You can take library books
home with you.

_____
_____

1. Some books have _____ in them.

_____
_____

2. Other books tell you about _____ .

Comprehension: Noting Important Details   CAROUSELS

● Read this story.

Henry wanted a dog.
Gramps told him all the things that
a dog would need.

"A dog needs things to eat," he said.
"A dog needs to go out for walks.
You will have to walk your dog
three times a day.
A dog needs a place to sleep, too.
I will help you make a doghouse."

● Print a word to complete each sentence.
For the last one, mark the space
for the answer.

_____

1. A dog needs things to _____ .

_____

2. A dog needs to go out for _____ .

★ A dog needs a place ____ .

◯ to swim   ◯ to sleep   ◯ to work

Comprehension: Noting Important Details

CAROUSELS

Houghton Mifflin Reading, 1989 Edition

● Print a word to complete each sentence.
Use the words in the box.

special	librarian
marks	authors

This rabbit is _____ .

The school _____ helps us
find books about rabbits.

We must not make _____
in any of the books.

Who are the _____ of
these books?

● Think about "A Special Place."

Read each question.

Underline the answer.

1. Who works at a library?
   a. Authors work at a library.
   b. Librarians work at a library.
   c. Curious George works at a library.

2. What order are the books in?
   a. The new books are first.
   b. The big books are last.
   c. The books are in alphabetical order.

● Print your answer to the question.

3. Why is the library a special place?

_____

_____

_____

_____

_____

_____

Comprehension: "A Special Place"

CAROUSELS

Houghton Mifflin Reading, 1989 Edition

● Follow these directions.

1. Take your pencil.
2. Draw a doghouse for the dog.
3. Find the name on the hat.
4. Write it on the doghouse.

Comprehension: Following Directions   CAROUSELS
Preintroduce the following new words that appear in the directions: *follow, directions.*

Houghton Mifflin Reading, 1989 Edition

19

1

- ○ money
- ○ mark
- ○ made

- ○ could
- ○ short
- ○ should

- ○ special
- ○ store
- ○ nothing

- ○ were
- ○ write
- ○ went

2

- ○ alphabet
- ○ again
- ○ after

- ○ room
- ○ roll
- ○ row

- ○ lost
- ○ listen
- ○ letters

- ○ order
- ○ or
- ○ once

3

- ○ us
- ○ use
- ○ has

- ○ begin
- ○ back
- ○ again

- ○ brown
- ○ brother
- ○ other

- ○ five
- ○ family
- ○ first

4

- ○ line
- ○ letters
- ○ last

- ○ of
- ○ or
- ○ row

- ○ raining
- ○ ran
- ○ thought

- ○ their
- ○ told
- ○ table

5

- ○ wait
- ○ water
- ○ write

- ○ happen
- ○ window
- ○ woman

- ○ very
- ○ every
- ○ crying

- ○ coat
- ○ both
- ○ boat

Vocabulary Test
Find number 1. Look at the words in the first box. Find the word *mark*. Mark the space for the word. (Continue in this manner, pronouncing the words to be tested.)

CAROUSELS

Houghton Mifflin Reading, 1989 Edition

1. jump ═══

_____

2. Henry is a good writer.   _____

3. The red house is bigger.   _____

_____

4. Reggie will paint the long fence.

       painted   painter

    _____

A _____ works hard.

● Read each sentence.

Print the word in heavy black letters.

Circle the picture that goes with the sentence.

1. She is a good **skater.**

_____

_____

_____

2. Reggie is a **runner.**

_____

_____

_____

3. This one is **harder.**

_____

_____

_____

★ Find the word that the *er* ending

was added to.

Mark the space for the answer.

Clara is a good **reader.**

◯ read
◯ rea
◯ reade

Decoding: Ending *er*
Preintroduce the following new words that appear in the directions: *added, black, ending, heavy.*

CAROUSELS

Houghton Mifflin Reading, 1989 Edition

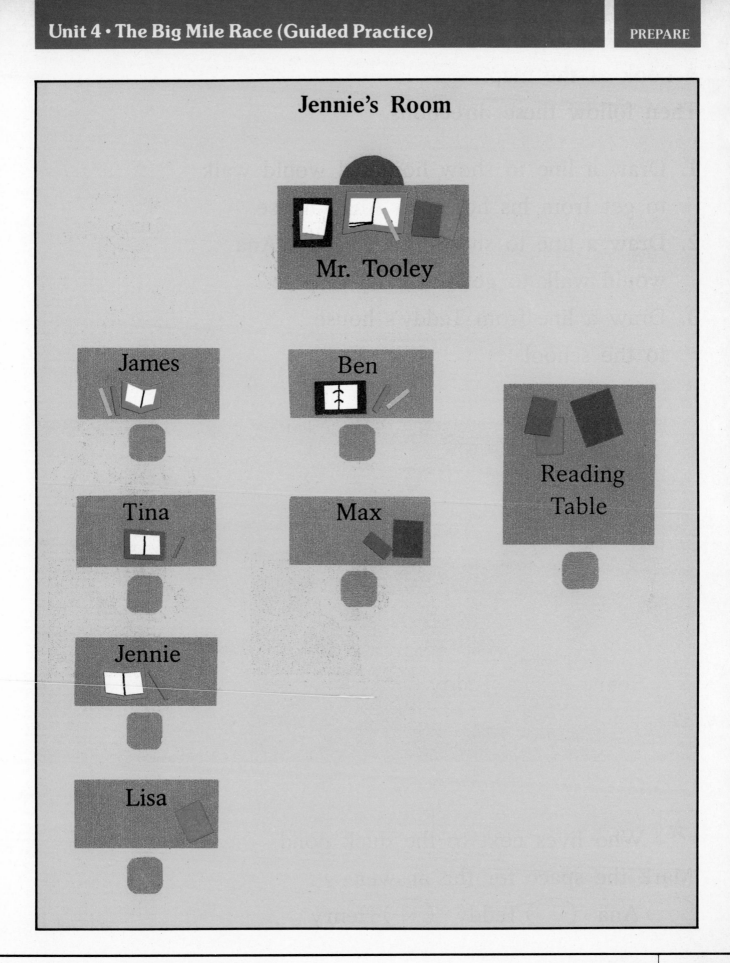

Jennie's Room

Mr. Tooley

James

Ben

Reading Table

Tina

Max

Jennie

Lisa

● Look at the map.
Then follow these directions.

1. Draw a line to show how Jed would walk
   to get from his house to Ana's house.
2. Draw a line to show how Jed and Ana
   would walk to get to Teddy's house.
3. Draw a line from Teddy's house
   to the school.

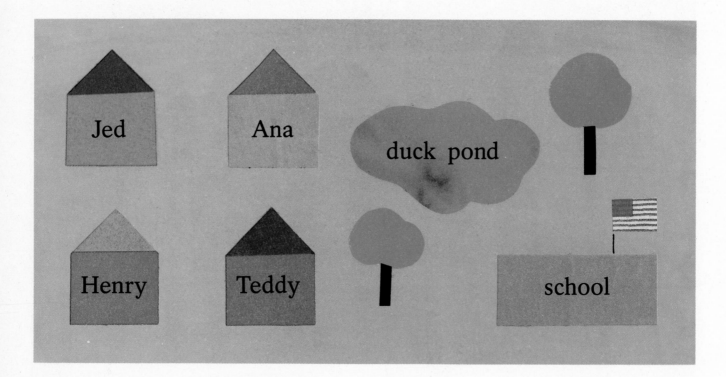

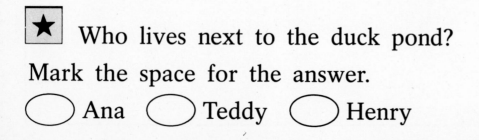

★ Who lives next to the duck pond?
Mark the space for the answer.
◯ Ana   ◯ Teddy   ◯ Henry

● Read each group of three sentences.
Decide which one tells about the picture.
Underline that sentence.

1. We are all ready to go out.
   We will all get ready now.
   We did not warm up.

2. "Let's race," said Owl.
   "Are you ready?" asked Goose.
   "Come on!" shouted Owl.

3. Cat runs a mile.
   Cat does not run at all.
   The rain comes down now.

4. Rabbit will finish first.
   Turtle will get to the finish first.
   Rabbit is warming up now.

5. Fox and Goose race.
   Fox has a race with Dog.
   Dog does not run.

Vocabulary: "The Big Mile Race"
Preintroduce the following new word that appears in the directions: *group*.

CAROUSELS

Houghton Mifflin Reading, 1989 Edition

● Think about "The Big Mile Race."
Read each pair of sentences.
Decide which one tells what happened first.
Put an **X** before that sentence.

Big Mile Race
Sign up today
at the tree
by the rocks.

1. _____ Rabbit and Turtle put up a sign.

   _____ Frog read the sign to everyone.

2. _____ Duck said that Frog would have to hop.

   _____ Frog said he wanted to be in the race.

3. _____ The racers ran every day to get ready.

   _____ At last it was the day of the big race.

4. _____ Everyone but Goose warmed up.

   _____ Turtle called, "One, two, three, GO!"

5. _____ At the pond, Goose stopped running.

   _____ Goose was fast but was slowing down.

6. _____ Dog got to the finish first.

   _____ One by one, the others finished the race.

| **Comprehension: "The Big Mile Race"**   CAROUSELS
Preintroduce the following new word that appears in the directions: *pair*.

Houghton Mifflin Reading, 1989 Edition

● Read each sentence and the words after it.
Underline the contraction for the words
in heavy black letters.
Print the sentence, using the contraction
in place of the two words.

1. I will show you the way.   **I'm**   **I'll**

_____

_____

2. We will go in here.   **He'll**   **We'll**

_____

_____

3. They will go to school.   **There's**   **They'll**

_____

_____

4. I am reading a book.   **I'm**   **It's**

_____

_____

Decoding: Contractions with *'ll, 'm*
Preintroduce the following new word that appears in the directions: *contraction.*

CAROUSELS

Houghton Mifflin Reading, 1989 Edition

27

● Look at the signs.

Then read each question.

Underline the answer.

A   BREAD FOR SALE

B   DON'T WALK

C

D   FISH FOR SALE

1. Which sign wants you to get a pet?

   a. Sign A   **b.** Sign D   **c.** Sign C

2. Which sign tells you not to do something?

   a. Sign A   **b.** Sign C   **c.** Sign B

3. Which sign wants you to get something to eat?

   a. Sign A   **b.** Sign C   **c.** Sign D

4. Which sign tells that you are coming to a hill?

   a. Sign B   **b.** Sign C   **c.** Sign D

Reference and Study: Signs   CAROUSELS

Houghton Mifflin Reading, 1989 Edition

1.

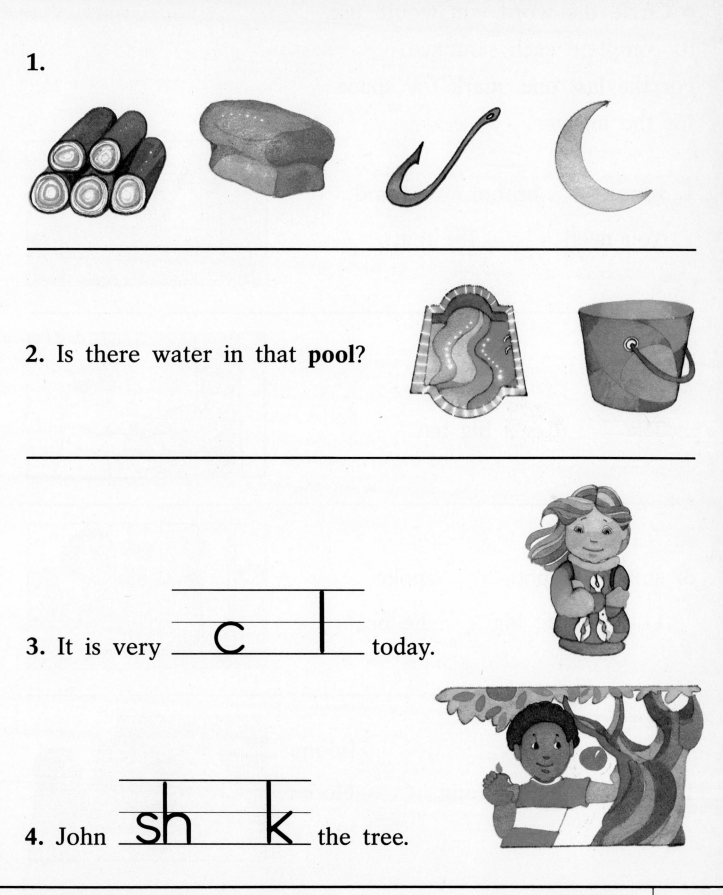

2. Is there water in that **pool**?

3. It is very ___ c ___ I ___ today.

4. John ___ sh ___ k ___ the tree.

● Circle the word you would use
to complete each sentence.
For the last one, mark the space
for the answer.

1. brook   broom   braid

You need a ____ for that.

2. cook   cake   crack

The ____ has a big hat.

3. spin   spoon   spoke

Look at the big ____ he has!

★

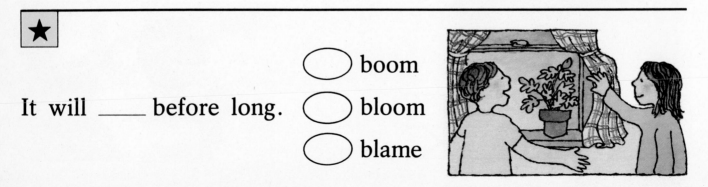

It will ____ before long.
○ boom
○ bloom
○ blame

Decoding/Phonics: Sound Associations for *oo*

CAROUSELS

Houghton Mifflin Reading, 1989 Edition

● Print a word to complete each sentence.
Use some of the words in the box.

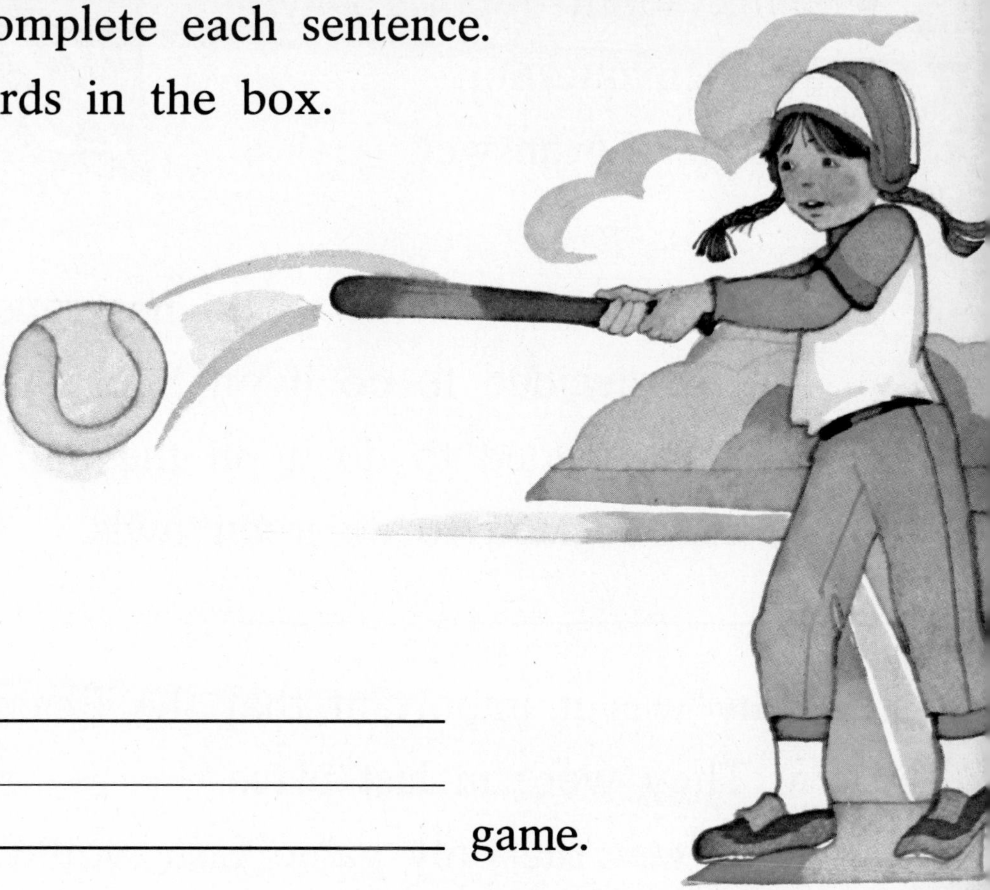

took	talk
sports	great
important	

_____
_____
It was an _____ game.

_____
_____
I _____ my bat.

_____
_____
I got a _____ hit!

_____
_____
Everyone will _____ about
this game.

● Think about "Sports Day."

Read each question.

Underline the answer.

1. What did Lisa decide to do her report on?

   a. Lisa decided to do it on Sports Day.

   b. Lisa decided to do it on the ball game.

   c. Lisa decided to do it on owls.

   _____

2. Why was it important that the Bears win?

   a. They were in last place.

   b. It was the only game Lisa would go to.

   c. A win would put the Bears in the first place.

   _____

3. Who hit a home run?

   a. Lisa hit a home run.

   b. Lisa's father hit a home run.

   c. Henry Wills hit a home run.

   _____

4. Who took a picture of Henry Wills and Lisa?

   _____

   _____

   _____

Comprehension: "Sports Day"   CAROUSELS

Houghton Mifflin Reading, 1989 Edition

● Read each sentence and question.

Print your answer to the question.

1. John is taking Teddy's dog for a walk.

　　　　_____

　　　　_____

Who has a dog? _____

2. Pam's pencil was in Mary's box.

　　　　_____

　　　　_____

Who has a pencil? _____

3. Ben wants some of Henry's sandwich.

　　　　_____

　　　　_____

Who has a sandwich? _____

4. Tina's cat ran up to Jed.

　　　　_____

　　　　_____

Who has a cat? _____

5. Jennie said she liked Reggie's picture.

　　　　_____

　　　　_____

Who has a picture? _____

Teddy

John

Teddy's Dog

1

- ○ bat
- ○ ball
- ○ brother

- ○ five
- ○ felt
- ○ family

- ○ again
- ○ give
- ○ games

- ○ her
- ○ held
- ○ hit

2

- ○ goose
- ○ grew
- ○ great

- ○ before
- ○ begin
- ○ both

- ○ three
- ○ talk
- ○ took

- ○ important
- ○ alphabet
- ○ sentence

3

- ○ every
- ○ ever
- ○ very

- ○ last
- ○ felt
- ○ fast

- ○ finish
- ○ first
- ○ four

- ○ has
- ○ happen
- ○ hill

4

- ○ kitchen
- ○ know
- ○ knew

- ○ map
- ○ mile
- ○ line

- ○ order
- ○ race
- ○ rocks

- ○ room
- ○ rest
- ○ rock

5

- ○ row
- ○ ready
- ○ rain

- ○ write
- ○ mark
- ○ warm

- ○ crying
- ○ slow
- ○ short

- ○ shouted
- ○ should
- ○ sound

Vocabulary Test
Find number 1. Look at the words in the first box. Find the word *bat*. Mark the space for the word. (Continue in this manner, pronouncing the words to be tested.)

CAROUSELS

Houghton Mifflin Reading, 1989 Edition

1.

_____ en

_____

2. I see a **wrinkle** here.

_____

wreck   rich

_____
_____

3. That boat is a _____.

wrap   wipe

_____
_____

4. Let's _____ this for Mother.

wing   wrong

_____
_____

5. That is the _____ ball!

● Read each sentence.
Find the picture that goes with it.
Put the letter of the picture on the line.

A

1. You put it on your **wrist.** ____

B

2. You need this to **wrap** things. ____

C

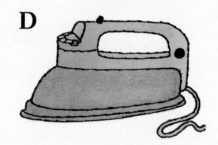

3. You can **wring** it out. ____

4. This gets out the **wrinkles.** ____   **D**

★ Read the sentence.
Mark the space for the word
you would use to complete it.

○ wrote

You are going the ____ way!   ○ wrong

○ wind

Decoding/Phonics: Sound Association *wr/r/*   CAROUSELS

36

Houghton Mifflin Reading, 1989 Edition

1.

2. Boo is a little dog.

He is Lisa's dog.

He jumps up every time
he sees Lisa.

Lisa is in school now.

She will be home soon.

Boo waits and waits.

At last Lisa comes home.

"Here I am, Boo!" she calls.

a. Boo will go to school.

b. Boo will jump up.

c. Boo will run home.

Comprehension: Predicting Outcomes   CAROUSELS

Houghton Mifflin Reading, 1989 Edition

● Read this.

Maria and Jennie were painting.
Beatrice thought painting looked like fun.
"May I paint, too?" asked Beatrice.

"If you go to the store for more paint,
then you can help us," said Maria.

Beatrice didn't want to go to the store.
"I could go home and play," Beatrice
thought.
"But I don't want to go home.
I want to paint with Maria and Jennie."

● Choose two sentences that help you
decide what Beatrice will do.
Underline those sentences in the story.

★ Mark the space for the sentence
that tells what Beatrice will do.

⬭ Beatrice will go home.

⬭ Beatrice will get some paint.

⬭ Beatrice will go out to play.

Comprehension: Predicting Outcomes
Preintroduce the following new words that appear in the directions: *choose, those*.

CAROUSELS

Houghton Mifflin Reading, 1989 Edition

• Print a word to complete each sentence.
Use the words in the box.

dear	move
love	wrote
share	

_____

_____

"It's time to _____," Fox told her friends.

_____

_____

"Oh, _____," said Frog, "we will miss you."

_____

_____

"Will you write to _____ news?" asked Turtle.

_____

_____

After she moved, Fox _____ letters
and drew pictures for her friends.

_____

_____

"My _____ to all!" she said.

Vocabulary: "We Are Best Friends"

CAROUSELS

● Think about "We Are Best Friends."
Read each question.
Print the answer.
Use the words in the box.

Peter   Robert

1. Who moved away?
_____
_____

2. Who thought Will was a silly name?
_____
_____

3. Who made a new friend named Alex?
_____
_____

4. Who showed Will where the frogs were?
_____
_____

5. Who went to Will's house to play?
_____
_____

● Read each sentence.

Print the word in heavy black letters.

Circle the picture that goes with the sentence.

1. He is a **mover**.

_____

_____

_____

2. She is the **batter**.

_____

_____

_____

3. He is a **swimmer**.

_____

_____

_____

4. She is a **worker**.

_____

_____

_____

5. He is a **reader**.

_____

_____

_____

● Read each question.
Underline the answers.

1. Which are rooms in a house?

    kitchen   bedroom

    playroom   doghouse

2. Which may be in a family?

    mother   father

    supper   sister

3. Which help you go places?

    jar   boat

    skates   rocks

4. Which are for counting?

    tree   one

    five   key

5. Which are sentences?

    I can run.   We play ball.

    talk race hop   Lisa wrote her name.

Comprehension: Categorizing

CAROUSELS

Houghton Mifflin Reading, 1989 Edition

1. ___ebra

2. pu___le

3. You can **zip** it.

4. It can **buzz**.

5. hero   zero

_____

_____

It is now _____!

6. frozen   frown

_____

_____

The pond is _____.

● Say the name for each picture.

Do you hear the sound for **z**?

If you do, circle the picture.

★ Mark the space for the number

whose name has the sound for **z**.

Decoding/Phonics: Sound Association for *z*
Preintroduce the following new words that appear in the directions: *hear, whose.*

CAROUSELS

Houghton Mifflin Reading, 1989 Edition

● Read this story.

Mrs. Lee has a flower garden.
There are all kinds of flowers
in Mrs. Lee's garden.
There are even little trees.

Mrs. Lee would like to win
a prize at the flower show.
She is trying to find
the right flowers to show.

● Print the ending of each sentence.

1. Mrs. Lee has a

_____

_____

_____ .

2. Mrs. Lee is trying to find

_____

_____

_____ .

3. At the flower show, Mrs. Lee wants

_____

_____

_____ .

Vocabulary: "Harriet and the Garden"
Preintroduce the following new word that appears in the directions: *ending*.

CAROUSELS

45

Houghton Mifflin Reading, 1989 Edition

● Think about "Harriet and the Garden."

Read each question.

Underline or print the answer.

1. Why was Harriet in Mrs. Hoozit's garden?

   a. She was running to get a fly ball.

   b. She was running after the dog.

   c. She wanted to get some flowers.

_____

2. What happened to Mrs. Hoozit's flowers?

   a. Someone gave them a prize.

   b. Nothing happened to them.

   c. Harriet messed them all up.

_____

3. Why did Harriet run away?

   a. She was scared.

   b. Her mother was calling her.

   c. She felt hungry.

_____

4. What did Harriet do for Mrs. Hoozit?

_____

_____

_____

● Read the story.

Then read each summary.

Circle the better one, **a** or **b**.

One day a fox fell into a well.

He could not get out.

Soon a bear came by.

"Is the water good?" asked the bear.

The smart fox got an idea.

"Yes, it is good," he said.

"Come down and swim with me."

The silly bear jumped into the well.

The fox hopped up onto the bear's back.

Then he jumped out of the well.

"Now how will I get out?" the bear asked.

"You should have thought of that
before you jumped in," said the fox.

a. A fox fell into a well.   **b.** Some animals were
   He got a bear to   in a well.
help him get out.   One got out.

Reference and Study: Summarizing   CAROUSELS

1.

2. Put the **bowl** on the table.

3. The picture is too _____.

4. Peter can see the c___n.

• Circle the word you would use
to complete each sentence.
For the last one, mark the space
for the answer.

1. low   bow   blow

Can you ____ it out now?

2. grow   gray   growl

These plants will ____ to be big.

3. gain   gown   grown

She has on a new ____.

★

The ____ will take some.   ◯ crowns
                               ◯ crows
                               ◯ crowds

● Read each question.

Look at each picture.

Then print the answers to each question.

1. Does Lisa have all
of the map or part
of the map?

_____

_____

Lisa has _____

2. Does Amy have
a yam or an orange?

_____

_____

Amy has _____

3. Do you think Harriet
will grow even taller?

_____

_____

Harriet will _____

Vocabulary: "What Can You Do with a Yam?"

Tell children that answers have been started to help them and that they should complete each sentence.

CAROUSELS

Houghton Mifflin Reading, 1989 Edition

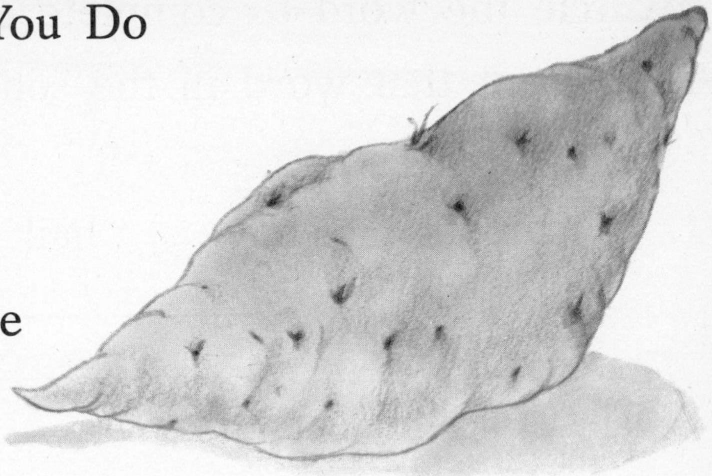

● Think about "What Can You Do
with a Yam?"
Print words in the lines to
finish each sentence.
The page number tells where
to find the answer.

1. To grow a yam, first put some warm water

_____

_____

_____ . (page 102)

_____

_____

2. Then push _____

into the yam. (page 102)

3. Next put the jar with the yam in it

_____

_____

_____ . (page 103)

● Now draw a picture of what
will happen to your yam.

● Circle the word to complete each sentence.
Then print that word in the sentence.

1.   carrots   hay   hail

_____

_____

They like to eat _____ .

2.   pay   pack   pain

_____

_____

Do you feel any _____ ?

3.   main   mail   pail

_____

_____

She brings the _____ .

4.   gray   white   grain

_____

_____

I like the little _____ cat.

1

- ○ game
- ○ gave
- ○ garden

- ○ dark
- ○ part
- ○ paint

- ○ ball
- ○ call
- ○ both

- ○ as
- ○ use
- ○ has

2

- ○ hot
- ○ hit
- ○ his

- ○ very
- ○ ever
- ○ even

- ○ finish
- ○ flower
- ○ family

- ○ stick
- ○ start
- ○ still

3

- ○ must
- ○ jar
- ○ just

- ○ ran
- ○ right
- ○ rocks

- ○ believe
- ○ before
- ○ begins

- ○ felt
- ○ four
- ○ from

4

- ○ last
- ○ love
- ○ vowel

- ○ mark
- ○ more
- ○ move

- ○ map
- ○ must
- ○ next

- ○ wrote
- ○ warm
- ○ write

5

- ○ ready
- ○ race
- ○ raining

- ○ told
- ○ talk
- ○ took

- ○ mile
- ○ line
- ○ mill

- ○ slow
- ○ shout
- ○ show

Vocabulary Test
Find number 1. Look at the words in the first box. Find the word *garden*. Mark the space for the word. (Continue in this manner, pronouncing the words to be tested.)

CAROUSELS

Houghton Mifflin Reading, 1989 Edition

1.

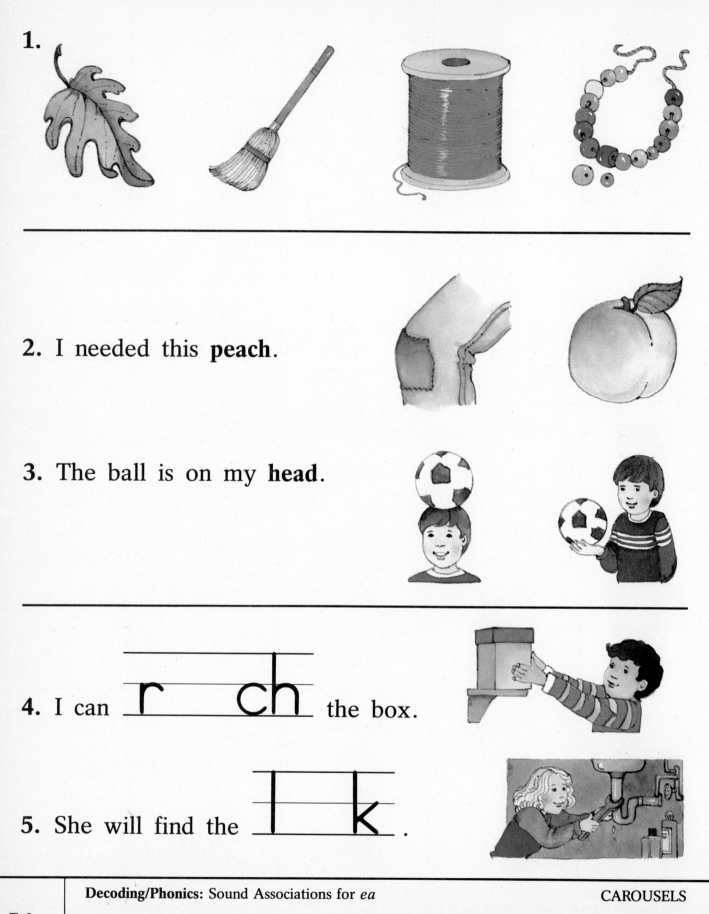

2. I needed this **peach**.

3. The ball is on my **head**.

4. I can r ch the box.

5. She will find the l k.

● Circle the word you would use
to complete each sentence.
For the last one, mark the space
for the answer.

1. meat   mate   met

I would like more ____, please.

2. states   seats   sails

Here are your ____.

3. tame   town   team

We are on the Bears ____.

★

This ____ is for you.
- ( ) scatter
- ( ) sweater
- ( ) sweeter

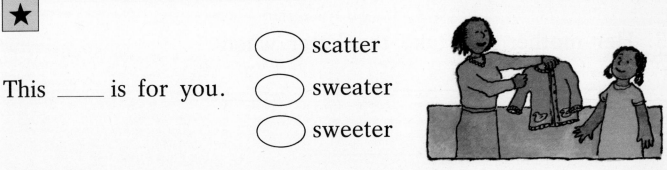

● Read this story.
Then print a word to complete each sentence.

Alma makes up stories in her head.
This story is about a detective
who has a hard case.
Her last story was about a dinosaur.
Alma is putting her story
in a letter to her friend.
She is putting a sticky stamp
on the letter.
Her mother will take the letter
when she leaves for work.

_____
_____

1. Alma makes up stories in her _____.

_____
_____

2. Her last story was about a _____.

3. Her mother will take the letter when

_____
_____

she _____ .

Vocabulary: "Nate the Great and the Lost Stamp" (Part One)   CAROUSELS

Houghton Mifflin Reading, 1989 Edition

● Think about Nate the Great.

Read each question.

Print the answer.

Use the words in the box.

Claude	Pip	Nate	Rosamond	Annie

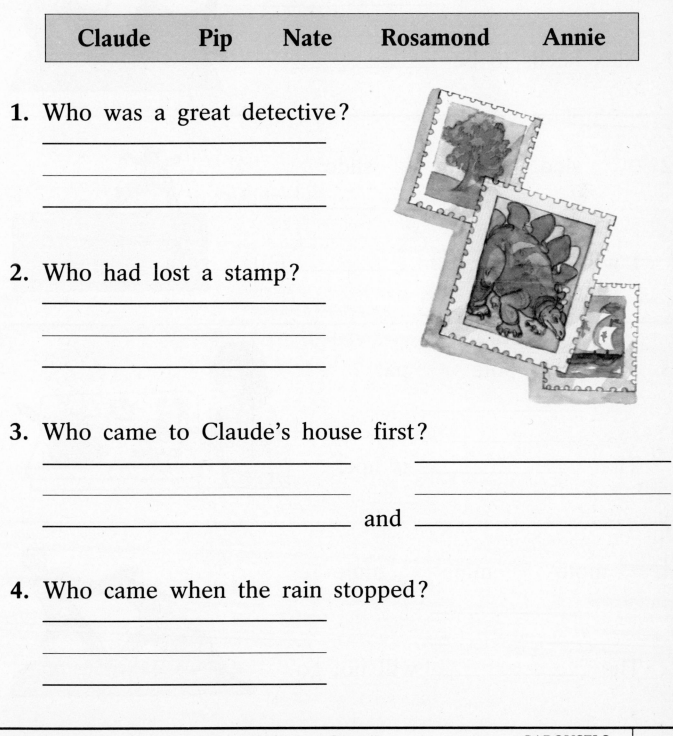

1. Who was a great detective?

_____

_____

2. Who had lost a stamp?

_____

_____

_____

3. Who came to Claude's house first?

_____   _____

_____   _____

_____ and _____

4. Who came when the rain stopped?

_____

_____

_____

● Circle the word to complete each sentence.
Then print that word in the sentence.

1.   fed   fade   free

_____
_____

Alex needs to be _____ .

2.   sled   slap   slide

_____
_____

I will go down the _____ .

3.   pot   pole   pat

_____
_____

That _____ is hot!

4.   mole   mine   mule

_____
_____

The _____ will not go.

● Look at the map.
Then follow these directions.

1. Rabbit is in the garden.
   Find the garden.
   Draw a line to show how Rabbit
would hop to get to the pond.

2. Draw a line to show how Rabbit
would get from the pond
to the fence.

3. Draw a line to show how Rabbit
would get from the fence
to her home by the tree.

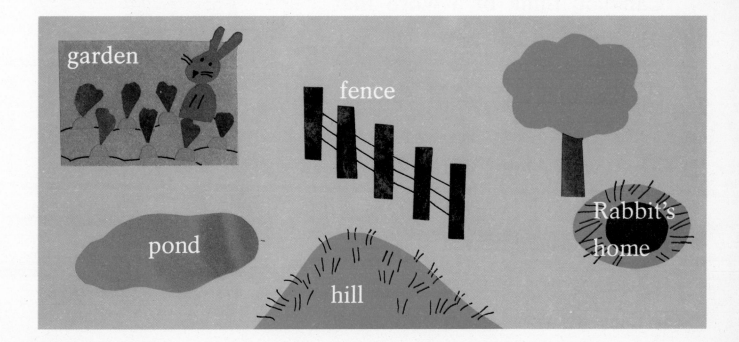

Reference and Study: Picture Maps   CAROUSELS

Mr. Mills was taking a walk.

He stopped by a big tree.

Something went "Whoooo!"

Mr. Mills looked up.

He was surprised by what he saw.

a tadpole   an owl

Alma wrote one line.

The last word she wrote was **cat**.

Then she wrote another line.

The last word in it was **hat**.

Alma looked up at her brother.

"Can you think of a word that sounds like **cat** and **hat**?" she asked.

"How about **sat**?" said Alma's brother.

1. What was Alma writing?

   a letter   a poem   the alphabet

2. How do you know?

   It uses words with the same sounds.

   It uses all the letters from **a** to **z**.

Comprehension: Drawing Conclusions

CAROUSELS

60

Houghton Mifflin Reading, 1989 Edition

● Read each story.

Annie went to get some books.
She got one book about kites and
another called *One Scary Night*.
Then Annie asked the librarian
to help her find a good book of poems.

● Underline the words that tell
where Annie was.

at a bookstore   at home   at a library

Max put down the saw.
"Boo will like this," said Max.
"This is a good place for a dog."

All at once Max had another thought.
"I will paint Boo's name
on his new home," said Max.
So Max went to get his paints.

★ Mark the space for the words
that tell what Max made.

◯ a sandwich   ◯ a doghouse   ◯ a storybook

Comprehension: Drawing Conclusions

CAROUSELS

● Read the story.

Then print the answer to the questions.

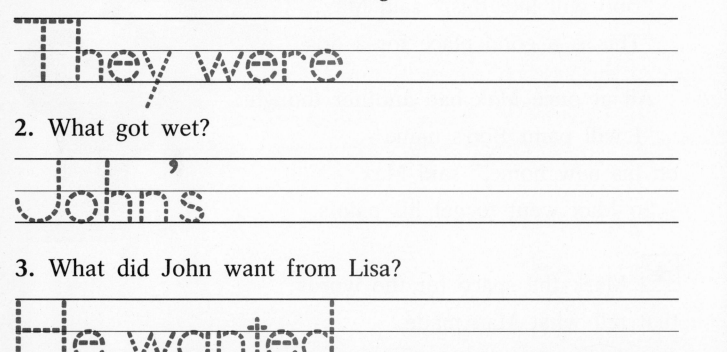

John and Lisa had been out playing.
The rain had stopped,
but there were still puddles.

"Oh, dear!" said John.
"My shoes are all wet!
I should not have walked
in all that water.
You won't need your slippers, Lisa.
May I put them on?"

1. What were John and Lisa doing?

They were

2. What got wet?

John's

3. What did John want from Lisa?

He wanted

Vocabulary: "Nate the Great and the Lost Stamp" (Part Two)

CAROUSELS

Tell children that answers have been started to help them and that they should trace over the dotted lines.

62

Houghton Mifflin Reading, 1989 Edition

● Think about Nate the Great.

Read each question.

Underline the answer.

1. What had Claude lost?

   a. one of his shoes

   b. a dinosaur stamp

   c. his little brown dog

   _____

2. Who had been at Claude's house?

   a. Annie, Pip, and Rosamond

   b. Rosamond only

   c. Annie and her dog Fang

   _____

3. Where did Nate find the missing stamp?

   a. on a letter

   b. in a puddle

   c. on Pip's shoe

   _____

4. Why did Nate ask to see Fang's smile?

   a. to find out what a dinosaur looked like

   b. to get his ball from Fang

   c. to get Pip's shoe away from Fang

Comprehension: "Nate the Great and the Lost Stamp"
(Part Two)

● Circle the word to complete each sentence.
Then print that word in the sentence.

1. growl   glow   gown

_____

This will _____ in the dark.

2. crown   crow   croak

_____

She has a _____.

3. town   towel   toward

_____

Will you give me a _____?

4. cloud   claw   clown

_____

Look at that _____!

● Read the words in each box.
Then print the words
in alphabetical order.

fish	can
ducks	eat

like	frogs
pond	water

1. _____

2. _____

3. _____

4. _____

1. _____

2. _____

3. _____

4. _____

● Read the sentences in each group.

Decide which one tells about the picture.

Underline that sentence.

1. Most of the boats are yellow.

   One boat is yellow.

   All of the boats look the same.

2. The boy has a yellow hat.

   The hat has a boat on it.

   The boy has a yellow boat.

3. The main part of this lunch is a sandwich.

   There are two sandwiches in this lunch.

   Soup is the main part of this lunch.

4. Two flowers are yellow.

   Most of the flowers are red.

   The flowers are on a boat.

• Read each story and the sentences below.
For the first one, underline the sentence
that tells the main idea.
For the last one, mark the space
for the answer.

1. Tadpoles grow up in a surprising way.
   They live and look like little fish.
   They have tails that help them swim.
   But tadpoles are not fish at all.
   They grow up to become frogs!

   a. They live and look like little fish.
   b. They have tails that help them swim.
   c. Tadpoles grow up in a surprising way.

★

Frogs live in many different places.
Some frogs live in or by water.
Others live where there is no water at all.
Some frogs even live in trees.

○ Some frogs live in or by water.
○ Frogs live in many different places.
○ Some frogs even live in trees.

Comprehension: Getting the Main Idea   CAROUSELS

● Read this.

Mary and Henry went to get a dog.
They wanted a dog they both liked.

First, Henry saw a dog he liked,
but Mary didn't like the dog.
"That dog is too little," Mary said.

Then, Mary saw a dog she liked.
Henry thought the dog was too big.

So Henry and Mary looked again.
At last they found a dog that was
not too big and not too little.
They both liked the dog.
The dog liked both of them.

● Circle the words that tell
what the children will do.
look again   get a cat   get the last dog

● Now find three sentences in the story
that helped you decide.
Underline those sentences.

Comprehension: Predicting Outcomes   CAROUSELS

Houghton Mifflin Reading, 1989 Edition

1

- ○ sail
- ○ smile
- ○ still

- ○ very
- ○ your
- ○ yellow

- ○ pushed
- ○ pens
- ○ part

- ○ move
- ○ most
- ○ just

2

- ○ main
- ○ must
- ○ map

- ○ both
- ○ been
- ○ even

- ○ dark
- ○ dinosaur
- ○ different

- ○ happy
- ○ hill
- ○ head

3

- ○ or
- ○ off
- ○ order

- ○ gave
- ○ sail
- ○ save

- ○ shoe
- ○ short
- ○ side

- ○ warm
- ○ wet
- ○ wrote

4

- ○ left
- ○ let
- ○ lick

- ○ give
- ○ love
- ○ leave

- ○ head
- ○ held
- ○ had

- ○ slow
- ○ mile
- ○ smile

5

- ○ should
- ○ same
- ○ save

- ○ next
- ○ most
- ○ note

- ○ sign
- ○ side
- ○ street

- ○ sticky
- ○ story
- ○ scary

Vocabulary Test
Find number 1. Look at the words in the first box. Find the word *sail*. Mark the space for the word. (Continue in this manner, pronouncing the words to be tested.)

CAROUSELS

Houghton Mifflin Reading, 1989 Edition

1. 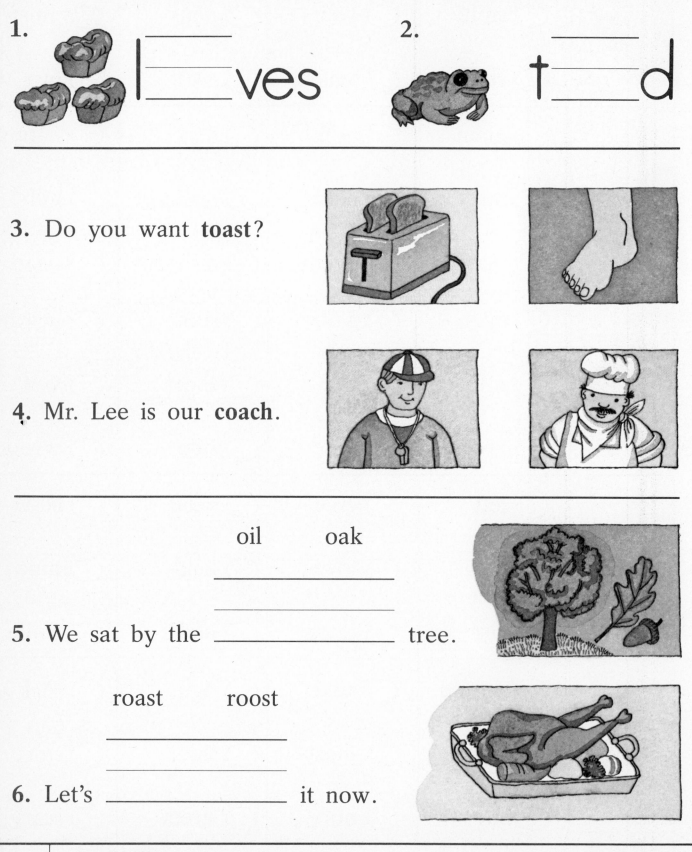 l___ves

2. t___d

3. Do you want **toast**?

4. Mr. Lee is our **coach**.

oil   oak

_____
_____

5. We sat by the _____ tree.

roast   roost

_____
_____

6. Let's _____ it now.

● Circle the word you would use
to complete each sentence.
For the last one, mark the space
for the answer.

1. flood   float   flat

I like to ____ on my back.

2. life   loop   loaf

Mother made a ____ of bread.

3. sad   soap   soot

The dog doesn't like ____.

★

Will the ____ come back?

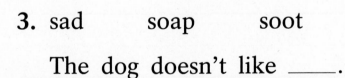

○ gate
○ goat
○ groan

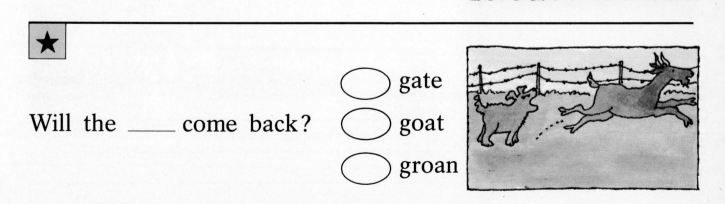

Decoding/Phonics: Sound Association for *oa*

CAROUSELS

● Print a sentence
to answer each question.
Use the word in the box.

1. Where is the goat in line?

second

_____

_____

_____

2. What kind of tree has needles?

pine

_____

_____

_____

3. What does a kite need to fly?

wind

_____

_____

_____

4. How does the fairy feel?

sorry

_____

_____

_____

● Think about "The Little Pine Tree."

Read each question.

Underline or print the answer.

1. Why was Little Pine sad?
   a. Little Pine had no friends.
   b. Little Pine wanted leaves.
   c. Little Pine wanted to be big.

2. What could Wind do to trees with leaves?
   a. Wind could make them sing.
   b. Wind could make them sick.
   c. Wind could make them brown.

3. What did Tree Fairy give Little Pine?
   a. Tree Fairy gave Little Pine slippers.
   b. Tree Fairy gave Little Pine needles.
   c. Tree Fairy gave Little Pine leaves.

4. What happened to Little Pine's leaves?

_____

_____

_____

Comprehension: "The Little Pine Tree" (Part One)   CAROUSELS

Houghton Mifflin Reading, 1989 Edition

● Read each question.

Look at the two pictures on the right.

Circle the one that answers the question.

1. Which is on **wrong**?

2. Which is **wrapped**?

3. Which is on a **wrist**?

4. Which is a **wreath**?

5. Which is a **wreck**?

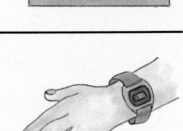

● Read the story and the question.
Then circle the answer to the question.

Annie put on her hat and coat.

She got her books and her lunch box.

When she looked out the window, Annie could see her friends waiting.

Annie said good-by to her dad and went out.

1. Where is Annie going ?

    to the store   to school   to eat

Peter put the plates on the table.

"What can I do now, Mom?" asked Peter.

"You can put the bread out," said Mother.

"Then I'll help you put the fish on the plates."

2. What is Peter getting ready to do?

    go to bed   go to the movies   eat lunch

Comprehension: Drawing Conclusions   CAROUSELS

Houghton Mifflin Reading, 1989 Edition

1. _____ock

2. _____ed

3. _____ove

4. You can find places on a **globe**.

5. Dad will **slice** the bread now.

blades   slides

6. Turtle sees _____ of grass.

broom   bloom

7. This flower will _____ .

● Circle the word you would use
to complete each sentence.
For the last one, mark the space
for the answer.

1. glass   blade   slant

You can put water in a ____.

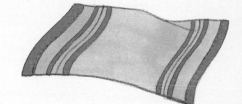

---

2. glitter   slender   blanket

A ____ keeps you warm in bed.

---

3. glide   slide   blind

You can have fun going down a ____.

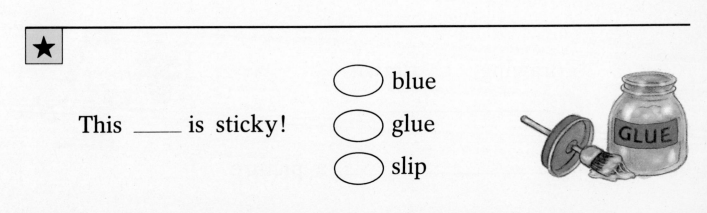

★

This ____ is sticky!

○ blue
○ glue
○ slip

Decoding/Phonics: Clusters *bl, sl, gl*

CAROUSELS

Houghton Mifflin Reading, 1989 Edition

1. blow ⎓⎓

2. eat ⎓⎓

3. Will you shorten these?

4. How that tree has grown!

darker   darken

5. I will _____ the room.

drawing   drawn

6. Pam has _____ a picture.

● Read each sentence.

Print the word in heavy black letters.

Circle the picture that goes with the sentence.

1. You need to **tighten** the line.

_____

_____

2. Her hat has **blown** away.

_____

_____

3. Have you **taken** one of these?

_____

_____

★ Find the word that the *n* ending was added to.

Mark the space for the answer.

Have you **drawn** a picture of me?

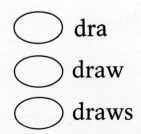

- ◯ dra
- ◯ draw
- ◯ draws

Decoding: *Endings en, n*

CAROUSELS

Houghton Mifflin Reading, 1989 Edition

● Read the questions.
Use the words in the box.
Then print the answers to the questions.
The first two have been started for you.

gold	glass

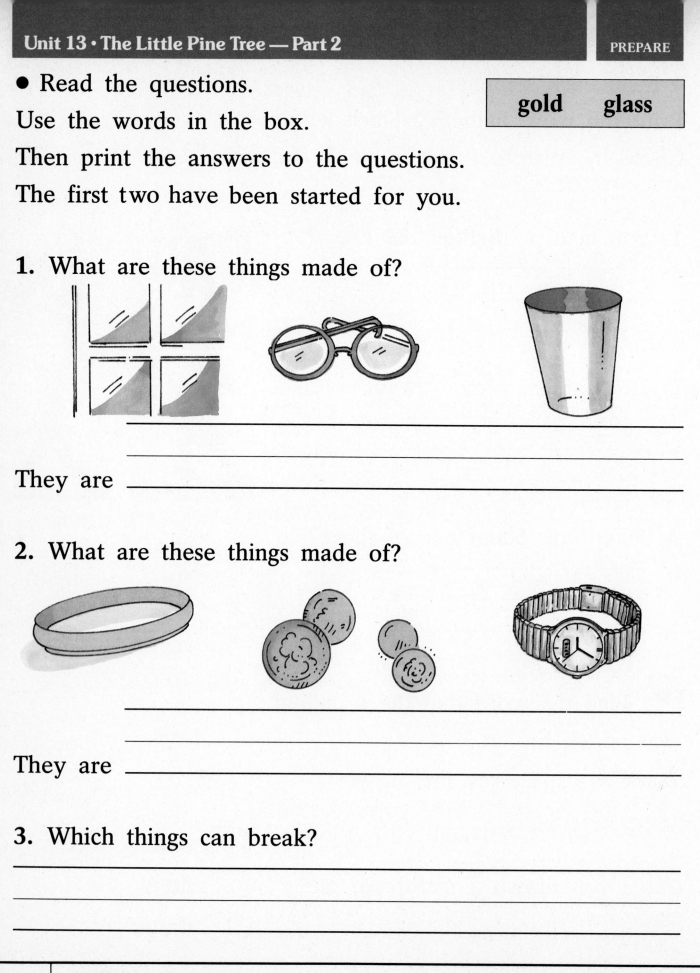

1. What are these things made of?

They are _____

2. What are these things made of?

They are _____

3. Which things can break?

_____

_____

_____

• Think about "The Little Pine Tree."

Read each question.

Underline or print the answer.

1. What did Wind do to Little Pine?
   a. Wind broke the glass leaves.
   b. Wind gave Little Pine some leaves.
   c. Wind ate all the leaves.

_____

2. What did Little Pine ask for next?
   a. Little Pine asked for sticky leaves.
   b. Little Pine asked for red leaves.
   c. Little Pine asked for gold leaves.

_____

3. Why did the man take the leaves?
   a. He wanted to make Little Pine feel sad.
   b. He wanted to give them to his brother.
   c. He wanted to get food for his children.

_____

4. Little Pine's last wish was for

_____

_____

_____ .

• Circle the word to complete each sentence.
Then print that word in the sentence.

1. brick brook broom

The ______________ is in the kitchen.

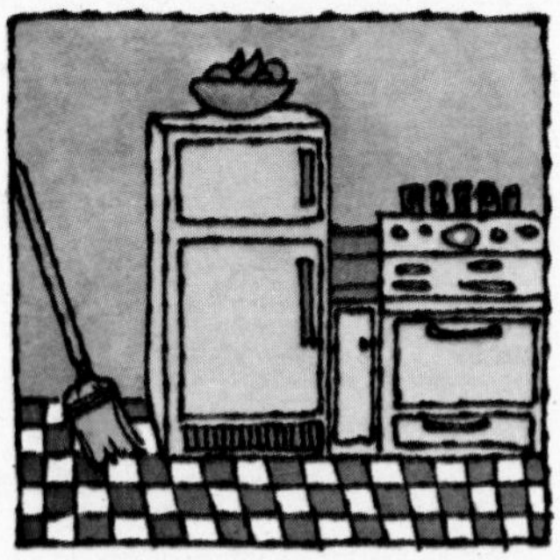

2. sun mood moon

You can see the ______________ now.

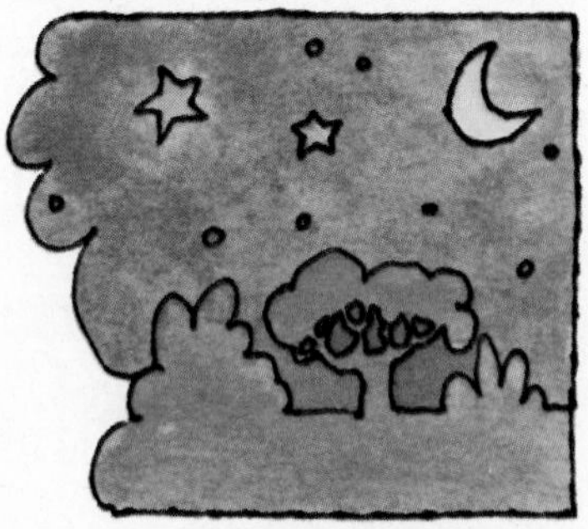

3. hook hood gloves

The ______________ will keep you warm.

4. spoon cool cook

Soon the soup will ______________.

Houghton Mifflin Reading, 1989 Edition

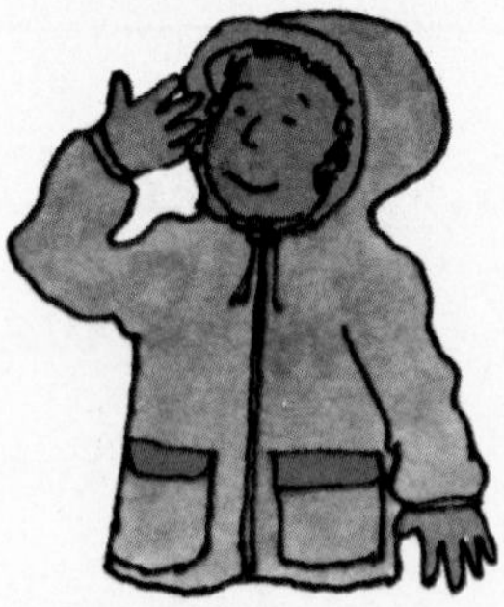

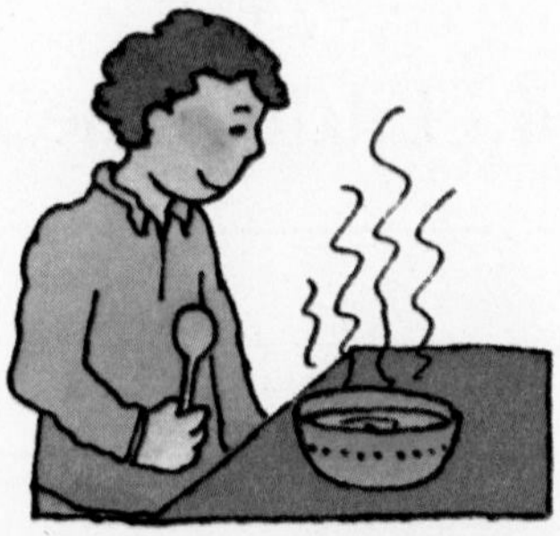

● Read the story.

Then print the person's name under his or her picture.

The children in my family like sports.

Each of us likes a different one.

_____
_____

Harriet is a great runner.

She likes to race, and she likes to win.

She works hard to get ready for a race.

_____

Robert likes to race, too, but not by running.

Robert is the swimmer in the family.

Sometimes I think he is part fish!

_____
_____

Nate likes to play ball.

He is a very good batter.

I have lost count of how many home runs he has hit.

_____
_____
_____

Comprehension: Noting Important Details
Preintroduce the following new word that appears in the directions: *person's*.

CAROUSELS

Houghton Mifflin Reading, 1989 Edition

1. "Where is the map?" asked Ana.

"I can't find **it**."

2. "We want to plant a garden,"
said the children.

"Will you help **us**?"

| her | it | them | us |

3. Look at **Susan!**

_____

_____

The coat is too big for _____ .

4. **George and Amy** are here now.

_____

_____

Let's go see both of _____ .

Comprehension: Word Referents *her, them, us, it*   CAROUSELS

84

● Read each pair of sentences.

Underline the words that mean the same
as the word in heavy black letters.
For the last one, mark the space
for the answer.

1. That woman lost her hat.
   I will run and give it to **her**.

2. Henry did not see the puddle.
   He skated right into **it**.

3. Annie and Will are going to school.
   Fang wants to go with **them**.

★ "Here comes Gramps!" said Ana and Alex.
   "He has some flowers for **us**."
   ◯ Gramps
   ◯ Ana and Gramps
   ◯ Ana and Alex

Comprehension: Word Referents *her, them, us, it*

CAROUSELS

Houghton Mifflin Reading, 1989 Edition

1. Reggie couldn't read.   Reggie broke his pencil.

2. Reggie couldn't write.   Reggie lost his storybook.

___

3. Ira saw the dog.
   It was a little dog.
   The dog looked hungry.
   Ira gave it some food.
   _____ Ira saw the dog.
   _____ The dog was little.
   _____ The dog looked hungry.

4. The table was a mess.
   It needed a coat of paint.
   Tina painted the table.
   Then she called Gramps to see it.
   Gramps thought the table looked
as good as new.
   _____ The table didn't look good.
   _____ Tina painted the table.
   _____ Tina called Gramps to see the table.

Comprehension: Understanding Cause-Effect Relationships   CAROUSELS

Houghton Mifflin Reading, 1989 Edition

● Read the story to answer the questions.
Underline the answer to the first one.
For the last one, mark the space
for the answer.

The race was about to begin,
and Lisa was ready for it.
She had run two miles every day.

The sign went up, and Lisa took off!
At first she let the other runners go by.
She knew that they could not run
that fast for very long.

When the time was right, Lisa ran
fast and went by all the other runners.
She was first over the finish line!

1. What happened to Lisa?
    Lisa was the winner of the race.
    Lisa didn't finish the race.

★ Why did that happen to Lisa?
    ◯ Lisa liked to race.
    ◯ The prize was a dog.
    ◯ Lisa worked hard and was smart.

Comprehension: Understanding Cause-Effect Relationships

CAROUSELS

● Read this story.
Then print the ending of each sentence.

It was raining.
Marvin Mouse got his blue umbrella.
On the way to school, he saw Tooley.
Tooley was a very shy grasshopper.
Marvin put his umbrella over Tooley.

1. Marvin has a big _____ .

2. His umbrella is the color _____ .

3. Tooley is a _____ .

4. Tooley is very _____ .

● Think about "What Mary Jo Shared."
Then print the words to complete each sentence.

1. At school Mary Jo wanted to

_____

_____

_____ .

2. First Mary Jo thought about sharing

_____

_____

_____ .

3. Then Mary Jo thought about sharing

_____

_____

_____ .

● Read each question.

Look at the two pictures on the right.

Circle the one that answers the question.

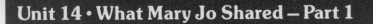

1. Which is a **zebra**?

2. Which has a **zipper**?

3. Which is **fuzzy**?

4. Which makes a **buzzing** sound?

5. Which is a **zoo**?

Decoding/Phonics: Sound Association for *z*

CAROUSELS

● Read each story.

Then read the sentences below.

Underline the one that tells the main idea.

1. The pine is a special tree.

It has needles, not leaves.

That makes it different from other trees.

A pine tree has needles on it all the time.

a. It has needles, not leaves.

b. That makes it different from other trees.

c. The pine is a special tree.

---

2. There are two ways to use an umbrella.

You can use an umbrella when it rains.

Then you won't get wet.

You can put up your umbrella when it's nice out, too.

That's how umbrellas were first used!

a. You can use an umbrella when it rains.

b. There are two ways to use an umbrella.

c. Then you won't get wet.

Comprehension: Getting the Main Idea   CAROUSELS

1. talking ________________ 2. stopped ________________

3. Jennie has sailed boats before.

We sail the boats now.

4. Robert writes with a pencil.

We all write words.

played pushed

5. He ________________ the box.

scaring smiling

6. He is ________________ now.

Houghton Mifflin Reading, 1989 Edition

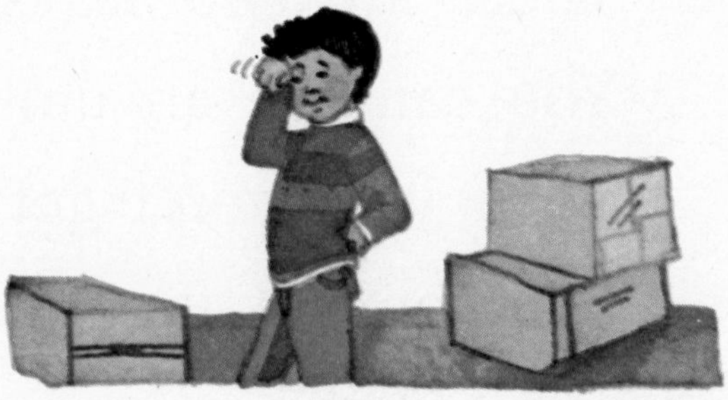

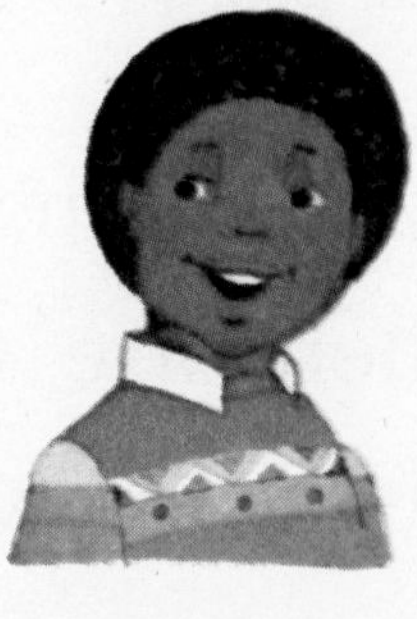

● Read each sentence.

Then print the base word

for the word in heavy black letters.

For the last one, mark the space

for the answer.

1. I have **taken** one.

_____

_____

_____

2. She **hopped** to the finish line.

_____

_____

_____

3. He is **baking** some bread.

_____

_____

_____

4. She **licked** the sticker.

_____

_____

_____

★ It has **holes** in it.

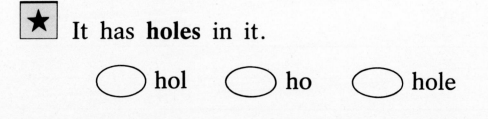

◯ hol   ◯ ho   ◯ hole

Decoding: Recognizing Base Words
Preintroduce the following new word that appears in the directions: *base.*

CAROUSELS

● Read this story.
Then print the answers to the questions.

It was a good day for sailing.
Gramps got into the back of the boat.
Then he helped Annie get in.

"Which way will we sail today?"
asked Annie, moving up front.

"The wind is coming from the west.
Let's sail with the wind," said Gramps.

"Off we go!" said Annie.

1. Where did Annie move?

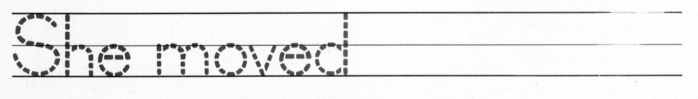

2. Which way was the wind coming from?

3. What did Annie say?

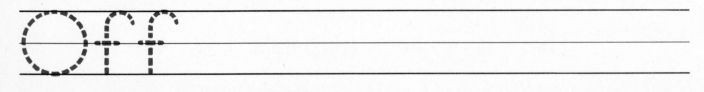

Vocabulary: "What Mary Jo Shared" (Part Two)
Tell children that answers have been started to help them and that they should trace over the dotted lines.

CAROUSELS

94

Houghton Mifflin Reading, 1989 Edition

● Think about "What Mary Jo Shared."

Read each question.

Underline the answer.

1. What was Mary Jo's problem?

   a. She didn't like her teacher.

   b. She didn't have a friend.

   c. She wanted to share something special.

2. Why didn't Mary Jo share her grasshopper?

   a. All the other children had grasshoppers.

   b. Jimmy had found three grasshoppers.

   c. She didn't want to scare the children.

3. What special thing did Mary Jo share?

   a. She shared her umbrella.

   b. She shared her brother.

   c. She shared her father.

4. Now all the children wanted to

   _____

   _____

   _____ .

Comprehension: "What Mary Jo Shared" (Part Two)   CAROUSELS

● Read each sentence.

Print the word in heavy black letters.

Circle the picture that goes with the sentence.

1. I need to **tighten** it.

_____

_____

2. Two of these have **grown**.

_____

_____

_____

3. One key is **golden**.

_____

_____

_____

4. One of these is **broken**.

_____

_____

_____

5. It needs to be **shaken**.

_____

_____

_____

Decoding: Endings *en, n*　　　　　　　　CAROUSELS

Houghton Mifflin Reading, 1989 Edition

1

○ held	○ front	○ write	○ blue
○ hand	○ food	○ wish	○ ball
○ happy	○ flower	○ west	○ blow

2

○ teacher	○ head	○ morning	○ felt
○ letter	○ holes	○ move	○ food
○ each	○ hill	○ main	○ fast

3

○ woods	○ been	○ great	○ wet
○ west	○ break	○ girls	○ when
○ wrote	○ believe	○ glass	○ wish

4

○ brother	○ gold	○ rocks	○ with
○ better	○ garden	○ before	○ warm
○ break	○ told	○ broke	○ wind

5

○ warm	○ bat	○ pens	○ smile
○ most	○ blow	○ pretty	○ second
○ man	○ told	○ part	○ sad

Vocabulary Test
Find number 1. Look at the words in the first box. Find the word *hand*. Mark the space for the word. (Continue in this manner, pronouncing the words to be tested.)

CAROUSELS

97

Houghton Mifflin Reading, 1989 Edition

1. cry _____

2. happy _____

3. Put the prettier plate on the table.

Both plates are pretty.

4. Bear tried to eat the hat.

Why did he try to do that?

5. That story is silly.

silly   sillier

_____

_____

This one is _____ .

Decoding: Changing *y* to *i* Before Endings

CAROUSELS

Houghton Mifflin Reading, 1989 Edition

● Read each sentence.
Then print the base word
for the word in heavy black letters.
For the last one, mark the space
for the answer.

1. The pig **tried** to do it.

_____

_____

2. The dog was **hungrier** this time.

_____

_____

3. The little boy **cried**.

_____

_____

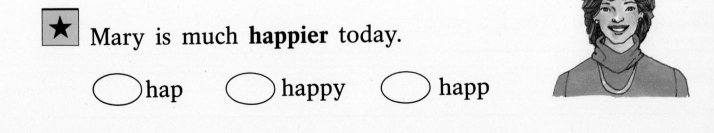

★ Mary is much **happier** today.

◯ hap   ◯ happy   ◯ happ

Decoding: *Changing y to i Before Endings*

CAROUSELS

● Read the words.
Then print the words in order
to make a sentence.

1. ugly drew an monster I.

_____

_____

_____

2. are lovely Monsters!

_____

_____

_____

3. you a make Will deal?

_____

_____

_____

4. people shy Some are.

_____

_____

_____

5. open you Are it's sure?

_____

_____

_____

Vocabulary: "Clyde Monster"

CAROUSELS

Houghton Mifflin Reading, 1989 Edition

• Think about "Clyde Monster."
Print the words to complete
each sentence.

_____

1. Clyde was scared of _____ .

2. Monsters and people made a deal

_____

_____

_____

_____

_____ .

3. An open rock would help Clyde

_____

_____

_____ .

● Read each sentence that tells what happened.

Then find the sentence that tells why it happened.

Print the letter of the **why** sentence on the line.

Why did that happen?

What happened?

____ Marvin ate everything on his plate.

____ Ann took her umbrella with her.

____ Ben jumped over the puddle.

____ Maria painted her room blue.

____ Tina made a doghouse.

____ Nate went to look for a pencil.

____ Beth took bread to the pond.

Why did it happen?

a. He didn't want to get his shoes wet.

b. She wanted to feed the ducks.

c. He was very hungry.

d. She thought it was going to rain.

e. He wanted to write a letter.

f. Her dog needed a place to sleep.

g. Blue was the color she liked most.

Comprehension: Understanding Cause-Effect Relationships

CAROUSELS

Houghton Mifflin Reading, 1989 Edition

● Read each pair of sentences.
Underline the words that mean the same
as the word in heavy black letters.

1. I am bringing back the books.
   I will put **them** on the table.

2. I wrote a poem for Mother.
   I will go and read it to **her**.

3. "Max has the ball," said Amy and Dan.
   "He is bringing it to **us** now."

4. Do you know where Lisa is?
   I want to show **her** what I made.

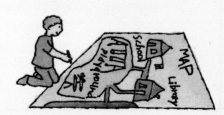

5. Nate is making a big map.
   He will take **it** to school tomorrow.

Comprehension: Word Referents *her, them, us, it*   CAROUSELS

Houghton Mifflin Reading, 1989 Edition

The story is about ＿＿＿ .

    a rabbit only   a turtle only   a turtle and a rabbit

It takes place ＿＿＿ .

    in a kitchen   in the woods   in a cave

● Read this story.

Then mark the space for the better summary.

A friend was coming to Harriet's home.

Harriet made some biscuits.

The biscuits were not the best she could make.

Out the window they went.

Then Harriet baked catfish and yams.

She was not pleased with them.

They went out the window, too.

When the friend got to Harriet's,
she was very hungry.

Harriet had nothing for her to eat.

Harriet said, "From now on, I will do
the best I can and keep the best I do!"

◯ Someone bakes biscuits, catfish, and yams.

Someone comes by and finds the food.

She thinks the food is the best ever!

◯ Harriet bakes food for a friend.

She isn't pleased with it, so out it goes.

When the friend comes, there is nothing to eat.

● Read this story.
Then print sentences to answer the questions.

Henry and Clyde were looking for Freckles.
They saw a squirrel and other animals
in the woods.
But they didn't see Freckles.

Then the boys saw a rabbit.
It ran into a hole in the ground.
Freckles was running after the rabbit!
"He'll never get it!" said Clyde.

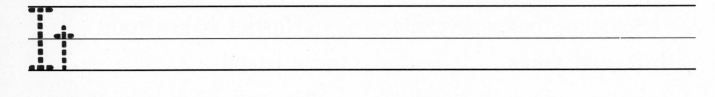

1. What animal did the boys see first?

They saw

2. Where was the hole that the rabbit ran into?

It

3. What did Clyde say about Freckles?

He'll never

Vocabulary: "Animal Houses"
Tell children that answers have been started to help them and that they should trace over the dotted lines.

CAROUSELS

Houghton Mifflin Reading, 1989 Edition

● Think about "Animal Homes."
Read each question.
Print the answer.
The page numbers tell where
to find the answers in your Reader.

1. What two animals live in caves? (page 204)

_____

_____

_____

2. What do bats do when it gets dark? (page 204)

_____

_____

_____

3. What two animals live in trees? (page 205)

_____

_____

_____

4. Where do moles live? (page 206)

_____

_____

_____

Comprehension: "Animal Homes"

CAROUSELS

Houghton Mifflin Reading, 1989 Edition

● Circle the word to complete each sentence.
Then print that word in the sentence.

1.   less   lash   leash

_____

_____

The dog has a long _____ .

2.   tease   toast   test

_____

_____

Jimmy will _____ the bread.

3.   coast   beach   skip

_____

_____

I'll _____ down the hill.

4.   load   dead   deer

_____

_____

This animal plays _____ .

Decoding/Phonics: Sound Associations for *oa, ea*   CAROUSELS

108

● Circle the word to complete each sentence.
Then print that word in the sentence.

1.   glad   mad   blank

    _____

Mary was _____ to see Gramps.

2.   gray   slacks   black

    _____

Look at the _____ cat!

3.   sling   sting   blink

    _____

Now Henry has a _____ .

4.   stove   glove   slant

    _____

Ana has only one _____ .

Decoding/Phonics: Clusters *bl, sl, gl*   CAROUSELS

1. push⸗

2. box⸗

3. Dan wishes his friend would come.

4. That's two misses for Tina.

fish   fishes

_____

_____

5. He _____ from the boat.

● Read each sentence.

Circle the picture that goes with it.

Print the base word for the word

in heavy black letters.

For the last one, mark the space for the answer.

1. He **mixes** the biscuits.

_____

_____

_____

2. She **pushes** the boat off.

_____

_____

_____

3. She **misses** this time.

_____

_____

_____

★ He **fishes** in the pond.

○ fishe

○ fish

○ fis

● Read the sentences in each group.

Decide which one tells about the picture.

Underline that sentence.

1. Grandpa scrubbed Rabbit's dirty ears.

   Mrs. Rabbit scrubbed her ears.

   Mrs. Rabbit fixed Rabbit's ears.

2. Mother lets Bear hold the shoes.

   The coat is not wrinkled.

   Mother lets Bear hold the wrinkled coats.

3. Nobody fixed the kite.

   Father scrubbed the kite.

   Mother fixed the kite.

4. Little Frog's shoes are dirty.

   Grandpa pulled Little Frog.

   Little Frog walked with Grandpa.

5. Grandpa will hold the glass.

   Baby Mouse fixed the glass.

   Mother says, "Never you mind."

Vocabulary: "Good As New"   CAROUSELS

Houghton Mifflin Reading, 1989 Edition

● Think about "Good As New."

Read each question.

Underline or print the answer.

1. Who is telling this story?

   a. Grandpa is telling this story.

   b. A boy named K.C. is telling this story.

   c. A boy named Grady is telling this story.

_____

2. What happened to Grady's bear?

   a. K.C. made a mess of it.

   b. It got lost in the woods.

   c. Grady's dog ate it.

_____

3. What did Grady want Grandpa to do?

   a. He wanted him to make K.C. help.

   b. He wanted him to go to the toy store.

   c. He wanted him to fix the teddy bear.

_____

4. What was the bear like when Grandpa finished?

   _____

   It was _____ .

● Read each sentence.
Circle the picture that goes
with the sentence.
Print the base word for the word
in heavy black letters.

1. Which dog is **dirtier**?
_____
_____

2. Which flower is **lovelier**?
_____
_____

3. Which bird **tried** to fly?
_____
_____

4. Which boy is **happier**?
_____
_____

1
- ○ or
- ○ arms
- ○ as

- ○ word
- ○ woods
- ○ food

- ○ flower
- ○ that
- ○ flat

- ○ hold
- ○ holes
- ○ hit

2
- ○ legs
- ○ letters
- ○ last

- ○ main
- ○ mind
- ○ most

- ○ pulled
- ○ pretty
- ○ special

- ○ than
- ○ talk
- ○ man

3
- ○ brother
- ○ book
- ○ break

- ○ birds
- ○ brown
- ○ break

- ○ glass
- ○ girl
- ○ ground

- ○ blow
- ○ blue
- ○ knew

4
- ○ very
- ○ never
- ○ next

- ○ order
- ○ open
- ○ pens

- ○ people
- ○ pulled
- ○ part

- ○ sad
- ○ sure
- ○ show

5
- ○ every
- ○ use
- ○ under

- ○ front
- ○ from
- ○ family

- ○ hold
- ○ hand
- ○ held

- ○ wish
- ○ when
- ○ west

Vocabulary Test
Find number 1. Look at the words in the first box. Find the word *arms*. Mark the space for the word. (Continue in this manner, pronouncing the words to be tested.)

CAROUSELS

Houghton Mifflin Reading, 1989 Edition

● Read this story.

Then print sentences to answer the questions.

"I have been meaning to call you," said Lee Mole.

"You left your hat at my house — the one with **L.M.** on it."

"That makes no sense," said Lisa Mouse. "I have a hat here in my hand. It also has **L.M.** on it."

"That must be my hat!" said Lee.

1. Who did Lee Mole call?

He called

2. What did Lisa say about leaving her hat at Lee's?

That makes

3. How is Lee's hat like Lisa's hat?

It also has

116

Vocabulary
Tell children that answers have been started to help them and that they should trace over the dotted lines.

CAROUSELS

● Read each sentence.
Circle the picture that is named
by the word in heavy black letters.
For the last one, mark the space
for the answer.

1. It feels hot by the **fire**.

2. Who is swimming in the **pool**?

3. The color of her coat is **green**.

★ He will eat the **carrot**, too.

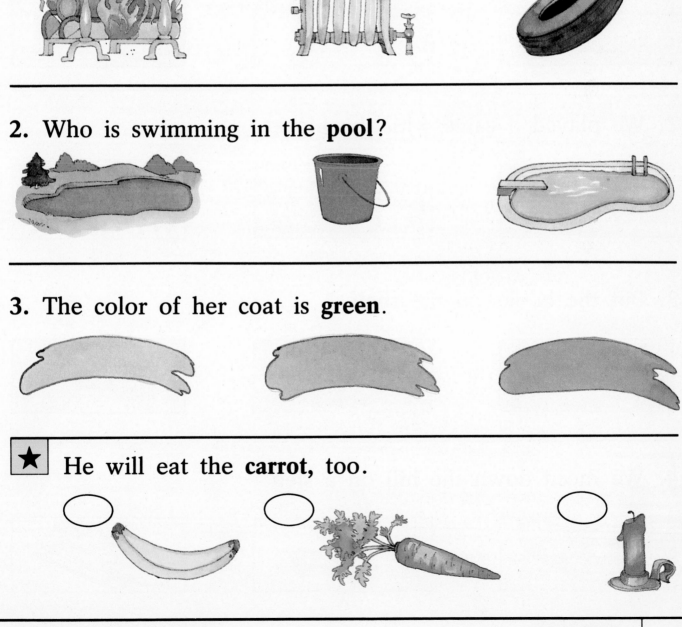

● Read each sentence.

The word in heavy black letters is new.

Use your reading skills to figure it out.

Circle the picture it names.

1. The children like to play in the **snow.**

2. We played a game with the **blocks**.

3. Put the books on the **shelf**.

4. We raced down the hill on a **sled**.

Decoding/Phonics: Using Letter Sounds and Context
Preintroduce the following new words that appear in the directions: *skills, figure.*

CAROUSELS

118

Houghton Mifflin Reading, 1989 Edition

● Read each question.
Circle the picture that answers it.
Then print the base word for the word
in heavy black letters.

1. Which one is **sadder**?
_____
_____
_____

2. Which one is **racing**?
_____
_____
_____

3. Which one **sailed**?
_____
_____
_____
_____

4. Which one is **dirtier**?
_____
_____
_____

Decoding: Recognizing Base Words   CAROUSELS

1.

2. Lisa **blew** them all out!

3. They ▢fl▢ here from their home.

4. Will the dog ▢ch▢ it up?

● Circle the word you would use
to complete each sentence.
For the last one, mark the space
for the answer.

1. curl   crew   chew

The ＿＿ is ready to fly.

2. blew   stew   sew

Grandpa makes good ＿＿ .

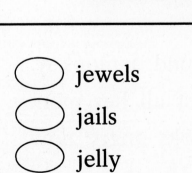

3. flew   free   flow

The birds ＿＿ away.

★

He wished for gold and ＿＿ .

◯ jewels

◯ jails

◯ jelly

● Read the sentences in each group.
Decide which one tells about the picture.
Underline that sentence.

1. Alma's old coat looks good.
   Alma wears her new coat.
   Alma's new coat is blue.

2. Robert threw the ball in.
   Robert threw the box away.
   Robert is very angry now.

3. Monkeys wear old coats.
   Monkeys live in trees.
   One monkey fell down.

4. Lisa found a monkey.
   Lisa lost all her money.
   Lisa looks angry now.

Vocabulary: "The Man and His Caps"

CAROUSELS

Houghton Mifflin Reading, 1989 Edition

● Think about "The Man and His Caps."
Then print the words to complete
each sentence.

1. The monkeys took all but one of

_____

_____ .

2. When the man shouted at the monkeys, they

_____

_____ .

3. When the man threw down his cap, the monkeys

_____

_____

_____

_____ .

● Look at the picture.
Read each question.
Print your answer.
Use the names in the box.

Frog	Rabbit
Mole	Duck

_____
_____

1. Who makes a sandwich? _____

_____
_____

2. Who mixes the biscuits? _____

_____
_____

3. Who messes up the kitchen? _____

_____
_____

4. Who fixes up the mess? _____

Decoding: *Ending es*   CAROUSELS

Houghton Mifflin Reading, 1989 Edition

● Read the sentences in each box.
Print the word or words
that mean the same as the word
in heavy black letters.

1. The boy broke his arm.
It will get better in time.
_____
_____
_____

2. Amy likes to feed the ducks.
She gives **them** some bread.
_____
_____
_____

3. "We are hungry," said the children.
"Will you make biscuits for **us**?"
_____
_____
_____

4. Clara likes that book.
Gramps will read **her** a story.
_____
_____
_____

Comprehension: Word Referents *her, them, it, us*   CAROUSELS

125

Houghton Mifflin Reading, 1989 Edition

1

- ◯ front
- ◯ flat
- ◯ foot

- ◯ happy
- ◯ arm
- ◯ angry

- ◯ off
- ◯ old
- ◯ woods

- ◯ top
- ◯ than
- ◯ told

2

- ◯ west
- ◯ wears
- ◯ ears

- ◯ left
- ◯ legs
- ◯ love

- ◯ morning
- ◯ meaning
- ◯ must

- ◯ wind
- ◯ man
- ◯ mind

3

- ◯ hold
- ◯ hand
- ◯ holes

- ◯ pretty
- ◯ pulled
- ◯ people

- ◯ also
- ◯ angry
- ◯ sad

- ◯ hand
- ◯ than
- ◯ head

4

- ◯ as
- ◯ angry
- ◯ arms

- ◯ birds
- ◯ blue
- ◯ broke

- ◯ begin
- ◯ kind
- ◯ knew

- ◯ never
- ◯ need
- ◯ next

5

- ◯ pens
- ◯ open
- ◯ old

- ◯ sail
- ◯ second
- ◯ sure

- ◯ under
- ◯ order
- ◯ use

- ◯ glass
- ◯ girl
- ◯ gold

Vocabulary Test
Find number 1. Look at the words in the first box. Find the word *foot*. Mark the space for the word. (Continue in this manner, pronouncing the words to be tested.)

CAROUSELS

Houghton Mifflin Reading, 1989 Edition

The House on the Hill

At last the house was finished.
Rooster got up on the very top.
He crowed and crowed and crowed.

Houghton Mifflin Reading, 1989 Edition

Pig had been living for too long
in a pen.

One day she said to her friend,
Sheep, "I don't like this pen.
I am going to build a house
on the hill."

And every morning Rooster crowed
to get the workers up.

Goose stuffed moss in the cracks
to keep out the rain.

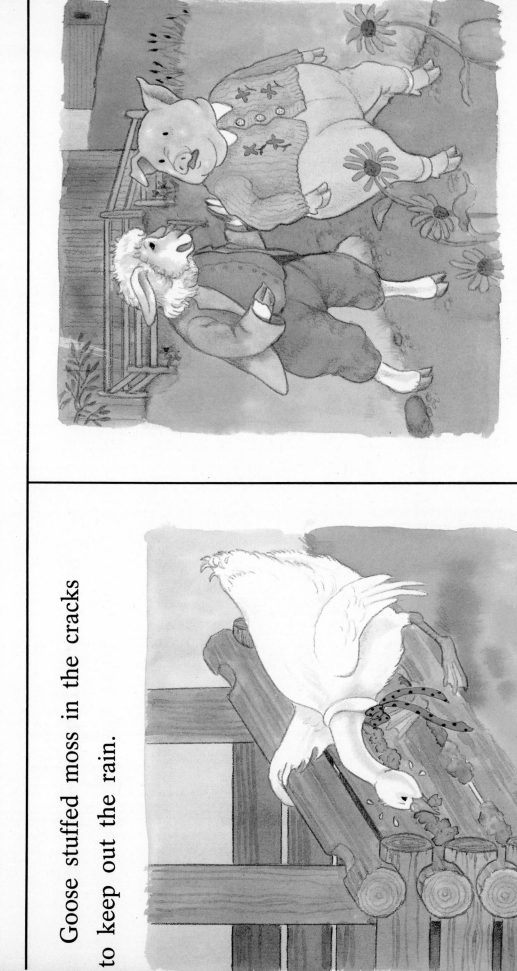

"Oh!" said Sheep.

"May I go with you?"

"What can you do to help?"
asked Pig.

Houghton Mifflin Reading, 1989 Edition

"I can pull logs for the house,"
said Sheep.

"Good!" said Pig.
"You are just the one I want.
You may go with me."

Sheep pulled the logs up the hill.
Rabbit made holes for the posts.

Houghton Mifflin Reading, 1989 Edition

17

Off walked Pig and Sheep.

As they walked, they talked about their new house.

Before long, they saw Goose.

Pig decided on just the right place for the house.

Then she found some logs.

Houghton Mifflin Reading, 1989 Edition

"Good morning," said Goose.
"Where are you going this fine day?"
"We are going to the hill to build a house," said Pig.

All the friends went to the hill.

"Oh!" said Goose.

"May I go with you?"

"What can you do to help?"
asked Pig.

"I can be your clock," he said.

"I will crow every morning

to get you up."

"Good!" said Pig and Sheep
and Goose and Rabbit.

"You are just the one we want.

You may go with us."

"I can find moss," said Goose.
"Stuffing moss into the cracks
of the house will keep out the rain."

"Good!" said Pig and Sheep.
"You are just the one we want.
You may go with us."

"Good morning," said Rooster.
"Where are you going this fine day?"

"We are going to build a house,"
said Pig.

"Oh, Oh, O-O-Oh!" crowed Rooster.
"May I go with you?"

"What can you do to help?"
asked Pig.

Off walked Pig and Sheep and Goose.

As they walked, they talked about their new house.

Before long, they saw Rabbit.

Off walked Pig and Sheep and Goose and Rabbit.

As they walked, they talked about their new house.

Before long, they saw Rooster.

"Good morning, Rooster," said Pig.

Houghton Mifflin Reading, 1989 Edition

"Good morning, Rabbit," said Pig.

"Good morning," said Rabbit.

"Where are you going this fine day?"

"We are going to the hill to build a house," said Pig.

"Oh!" said Rabbit with a hop.

"May I go with you?"

"What can you do to help?" asked Pig.

"I can make holes for the posts of your house," said Rabbit.

"Good!" said Pig and Sheep and Goose.

"You are just the one we want. You may go with us."